# CAN YOU COUNT TO A GOOGOL?

## Robert E. Wells

Albert Whitman & Company
Chicago, Illinois

For my nieces, Susannah and Anna,
and my nephews, John, Nathaniel, Brady, and Austin.
May the new millennium bring you googols of blessings!

## Also by Robert E. Wells

*Can We Share the World with Tigers?*
*Did a Dinosaur Drink This Water?*
*How Do You Know What Time It Is?*
*How Do You Lift a Lion?*
*Is a Blue Whale the Biggest Thing There Is?*
*Polar Bear, Why Is Your World Melting?*
*What's Faster Than a Speeding Cheetah?*
*What's Older Than a Giant Tortoise?*
*What's Smaller Than a Pygmy Shrew?*
*What's So Special about Planet Earth?*
*Why Do Elephants Need the Sun?*

Library of Congress Cataloging-in-Publication Data

Wells, Robert E.
Can you count to a googol? / Robert E. Wells
p. cm.
1. Decimal system—Juvenile literature. 2. Multiplication—Juvenile literature.
[1. Decimal system. 2. Multiplication.] I. Title.
QA141.35.W45    2000    98-49759    513.5'5—dc21    CIP    AC

Text and illustrations copyright © 2000 by Robert E. Wells
Published in 2000 by Albert Whitman & Company
ISBN 978-0-8075-1061-2

Printed in China
24 23 22 21 20 19 NP 22 21 20 19 18 17

Hand lettering by Robert E. Wells
The illustration media are pen and acrylic.
Design by Susan B. Cohen

For more information about Albert Whitman & Company,
visit our website at www.albertwhitman.com.

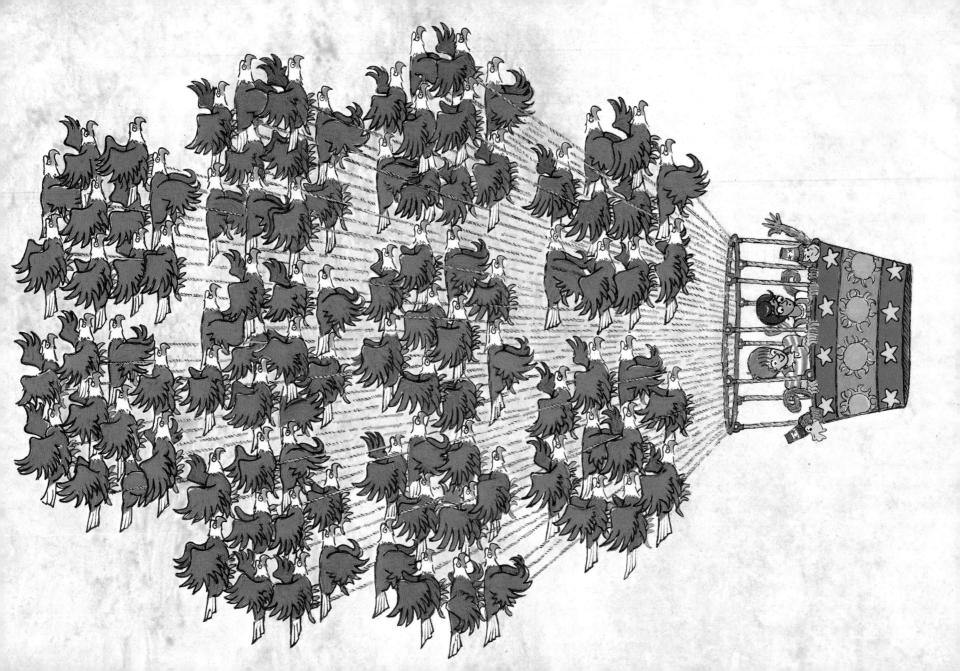

Perhaps 100 eagles could take you on a scenic ride high in the sky, if they were willing.

But, if you're searching for a really, REALLY big number, you still have a VERY long way to go!

# $10 \times 100$ is $1,000$.

If ONE HUNDRED penguins each had TEN scoops of ice cream in a cone,

that would be ONE THOUSAND scoops of ice cream.
ONE THOUSAND is starting to get big.

But don't stop there!

10 × 10,000 is 100,000.

If you had ONE HUNDRED THOUSAND marshmallows, you could put them into ONE HUNDRED baskets, ONE THOUSAND marshmallows in each basket.

Yes, you COULD say 100,000 is VERY big — especially if you had to eat that many marshmallows.

But...

ONE MILLION is 10 times bigger!
It looks like this: 1,000,000.

Sometimes, great
distances are easier to
measure in MILLIONS,
such as

the distance between the earth and the sun.

That's about 93 MILLION miles.

150 MILLION kilometers.

A MILLION is also useful for measuring long periods of time, such as the number of years that have passed since dinosaurs last roamed the earth. That's been about 65 MILLION years.

If you put ONE MILLION dollar bills in a money stacking and packing machine,

or, ONE HUNDRED MILLION dollars.

A BILLION is a MIGHTY big number. But, of course, TEN BILLION is TEN TIMES BIGGER!

It looks like this:
10,000,000,000.

Some stars in our Milky Way Galaxy are TEN BILLION years old.

Our SUN is a star. It's not that old yet, but someday it might be. It began to form about 5 BILLION years ago and will probably last at least 5 BILLION MORE years!

10 × 10,000,000,000 is 100,000,000,000, or, ONE HUNDRED BILLION. That's a TREMENDOUS number. But, as tremendous as it is, there are MORE than that many stars in our galaxy! Here are a few of them.

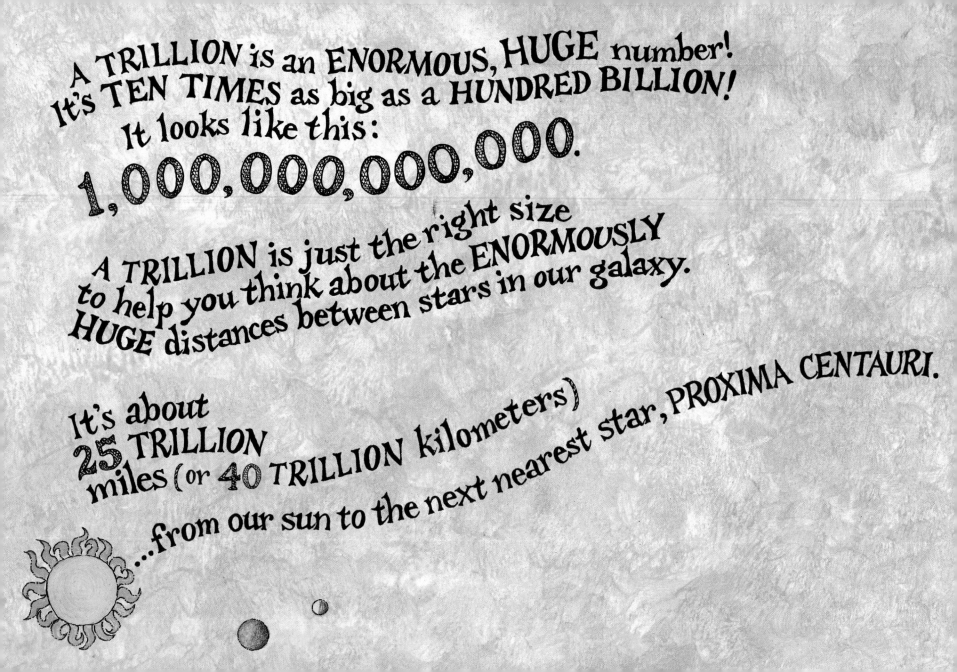

A TRILLION is an ENORMOUS, HUGE number!
It's TEN TIMES as big as a HUNDRED BILLION!
It looks like this:

1,000,000,000,000.

A TRILLION is just the right size
to help you think about the ENORMOUSLY
HUGE distances between stars in our galaxy.

It's about
25 TRILLION
miles (or 40 TRILLION kilometers)
...from our sun to the next nearest star, PROXIMA CENTAURI.

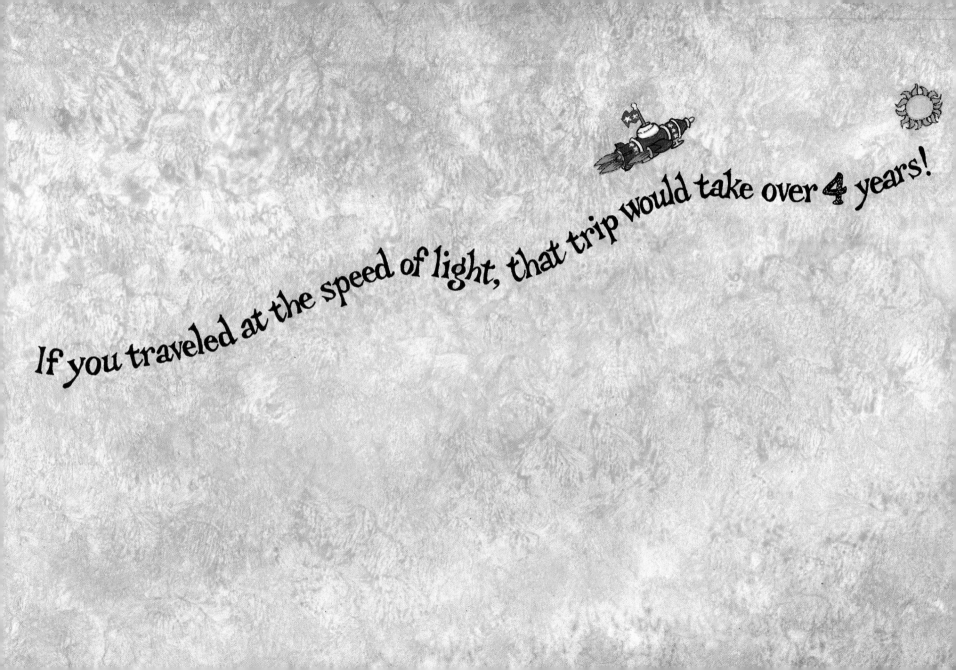

If you traveled at the speed of light, that trip would take over 4 years!

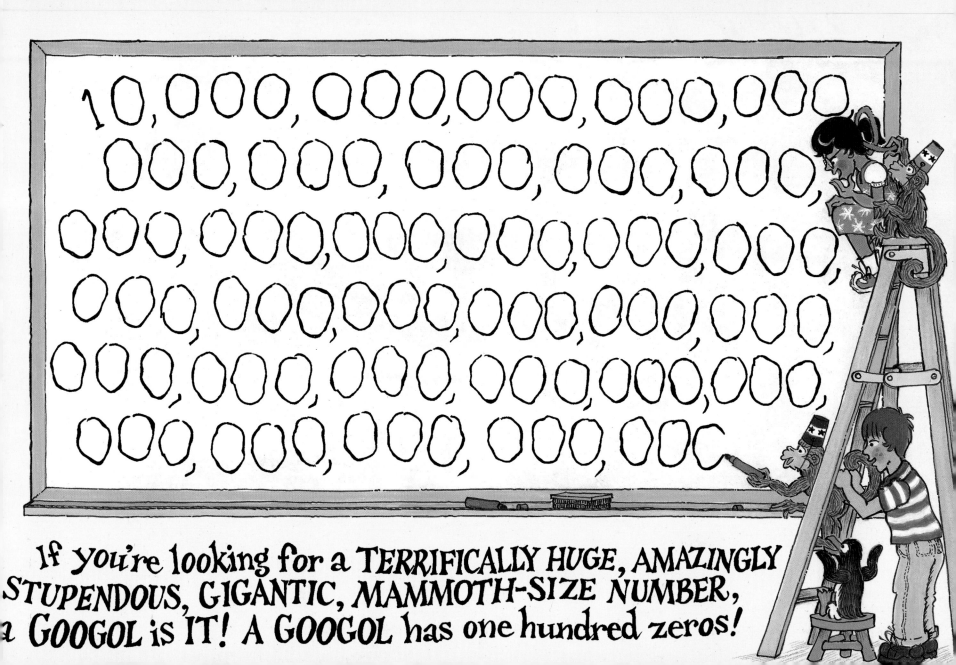

If you're looking for a TERRIFICALLY HUGE, AMAZINGLY STUPENDOUS, GIGANTIC, MAMMOTH-SIZE NUMBER, a GOOGOL is IT! A GOOGOL has one hundred zeros!

If you kept on counting till you'd counted every star, planet, moon, comet, and asteroid in our whole galaxy, that number STILL would be much smaller than a GOOGOL!

There's no use trying to count to a googol. It's just too big! A googol is BIGGER THAN THE NUMBER OF ATOMS IN THE WHOLE UNIVERSE!

00,000,000,000,000,000,000,000,000,000,000,000,000,000,000,000,

Did you ever wonder
just how far FOREVER is?

1,000,000 WOULD BE 100 STACKS. IN 10 ROWS OF 10, THEY'D MEASURE ABOUT

26 INCHES (66 CENTIMETERS) WIDE, 40 INCHES (1 METER) HIGH, AND 5 FEET (1½ METERS) LONG.

HOW LONG WOULD IT TAKE YOU TO SPEND $1,000,000?

OUR SUN

THIS MEANS WE CAN FIND THE APPROXIMATE DISTANCE BY MULTIPLYING 6 TRILLION (FOR MILES) OR 10 TRILLION (FOR KILOMETERS) BY 4¼. CAN YOU FIGURE OUT THIS APPROXIMATE DISTANCE?

PROXIMA CENTAURI

THAT MEANS 10 EAGLES COULD PROBABLY CARRY A 30-POUND (14-KILOGRAM) FISH.

SO — COULD 100 EAGLES TAKE YOU FOR A RIDE — IF THEY WERE WILLING?

# Yes, a Googol *Is* a Real Number!

One day in the late 1930s, Dr. Edward Kasner, an American mathematician, wrote down a number with 100 zeros. He didn't know what to call it, so he asked his nine-year-old nephew, Milton, to give it a name. Milton called it a googol— and so, on that day, a googol was born.

Over the years, the googol has captured the imagination of those who are fascinated by very big numbers. But just how big *is* a googol?

With observations and calculations, astronomers can estimate how many atoms there are in all the billions of galaxies in the known universe, and in all the space between those galaxies. Some astronomers estimate that if you could count all those atoms, that number would be at least $10^{80}$—or, a one followed by 80 zeros. But a googol, with 100 zeros, is one hundred million trillion times bigger than that!

Of course, it's almost impossible to imagine such a big number. But isn't it kind of fun to try?